To each and every EXPERT — to those parents, educators, librarians, children's book authors, child-development specialists, pediatricians, adult physicians, child psychologists, child analysts, and family and friends who read and looked over our work, talked to us, taught us, and helped us in so many ways over and over again as we created this book. We could not have done this book without you. And we certainly could not have created this book without the endless work and full support of our magnificent colleagues at Candlewick Press. THANK YOU TO ALL OF YOU! — R. H. H.

First edition 2016

Library of Congress Catalog Card Number 2015933255
ISBN 978-0-7636-6903-4

23 24 25 26 27 APS 11 10 9 8 7 6

Printed in Humen, Dongguan, China

This book was typeset in Berkeley Old Style.
The illustrations were created digitally.

Candlewick Press
99 Dover Street
Somerville, Massachusetts 02144

visit us at www.candlewick.com

Who We Are!

All About
Being the Same and Being Different

Robie H. Harris

illustrated by Nadine Bernard Westcott

CANDLEWICK PRESS

All around the world there are people—billions of people. But there is only one of you.

No matter where you go or where you live, no one else is exactly like you. And no one else looks exactly like you— not even the people in your own family, or the people who live where you live, or eat the foods you eat, or wear clothes like you wear, or go to the same playground you go to.

People can look a lot alike, but not exactly alike. Or not alike at all. Even twins whose faces and bodies look exactly alike may wear different hats, or shoes, or T-shirts or may have different haircuts. These kinds of things can make them look not quite exactly alike.

People's bodies are mostly the same—except for the private parts we are born with. Those parts are called a vagina or a penis.

Inside our bodies, everybody has a brain, a heart, a stomach, muscles, bones—and so many other parts that are the same for everyone. On the outside of our bodies, everybody has skin, a head, a nose, a mouth, fingernails, a belly button—and many other parts that are the same for most everyone.

Even the parts of our bodies that are the same can look different. People have different-shaped bodies, different-shaped heads, ears, eyes, noses, mouths—and even fingers and toes.

Some people are shorter. Some are taller. And some are in between. Some people have small feet and some have bigger feet. Some people have long hair and some have shorter hair. These are some of the things that make us look different from one another.

People have different colors and shades of hair. Some people's hair is brown or blond or red. Some people's hair is black or gray or white.

People also have different kinds of hair. Some people's hair is curly or very curly. Some people's hair is wavy or very wavy. And some people's hair is straight. Some people have lots of hair, or just a little bit of hair, or no hair at all.

People also have different colors and shades of skin. Some people's skin is darker and some is lighter. And some is in between.

There are many different names for all the different colors and shades of skin—names like coffee, cream, pink, black, honey, chocolate, gold, almond, ivory, brown, olive, white, cinnamon, bronze, and peach.

My skin's the same shade as honey.

My skin's the color of cinnamon. And baby Jake's skin is peach.

People's eyes have different shapes. Some people's eyes are oval. Some are round. Some are narrower. Some are wider. Some are big. And some are small. People's eyes can also be different colors—blue, or gray, or green, or brown, or hazel, which is green and brown mixed together.

Some of my friends wear glasses. They look really awesome.

Some people need to wear glasses to help them see better. Some do not. People also wear glasses to help protect their eyes from the sun. And many wear goggles when they swim to help protect their eyes and to see better underwater.

Sunglasses look really cool. When it's sunny, I wear sunglasses.

Everybody's skin, hair, and eyes contain melanin. The different colors of melanin—red, blond, brown, black, and mixtures of these colors—are what give our skin, hair, and eyes their color. If the color of melanin in a person's skin is darker, their skin color will be darker. If the color of melanin in a person's skin is lighter, their skin color will be lighter.

In our family, Daddy's skin is lighter. I think his skin looks like cream.

And Mommy's skin is darker. I think her skin looks like coffee.

Melanin that is darker can help protect our skin from getting too much sun. But too much sun can damage our skin. So no matter what color or shade our skin is— lighter or darker—when we are out in the sun, we need to put on sunblock and wear a hat so that we do not get too much sun on our skin.

The melanin in the round part of our eyes—called the iris—has color in it. The color of melanin in your iris is what gives your iris its color. If the color of melanin in a person's iris is lighter, their eye color will be lighter. If the color of melanin in a person's iris is darker, their eye color will be darker.

The color of melanin you have in your hair is what gives your hair its color. If the color of melanin in a person's hair is darker, their hair color will be darker. If the color of melanin in a person's hair is lighter, their hair color will be lighter.

Guess what, Nellie? You and Jake and I all have brown eyes.

Guess what else, Gus? My hair's darker than your hair. And your hair's darker than Jake's hair.

FUN PHOTO

Many things are passed on to us from our birth parents or birth grandparents, or even our birth great-grandparents. The color or shade of our skin or hair, the color or shape of our eyes, how tall we are, or the way we smile, are some of the things that were passed on to us.

That's why you may have a nose that looks like one of your birth parents' noses, hair that looks like the other birth parent's hair, or skin that looks like a mixture of both of them. Or these things may have been passed on to you from your birth grandparents or birth great-grandparents. Some other things that may have been passed on by the family you live with are the way you laugh, the foods you like to eat, or the games you like to play.

How a person walks or talks, or the clothes a person wears, or the color or shade of their skin, hair, or eyes can't tell you what a person is really like. The holidays a person celebrates, or the people in a person's family, or the foods a person eats also can't tell you what a person is really like. That person may be a lot like you in some ways and different from you in other ways.

You may have freckles. Another person may not. That person may speak Spanish. You may not. You may use crutches or a wheelchair. Another person may not. That person may like to sing. You may like to tell jokes. Or both of you may wear orange sneakers. Or have the same backpack. Or have brown eyes. Or curly hair.

When you meet another kid for the first time, you may want to play with that person right away. Or you may not want to because he or she is someone you have never met or seen before. You may feel curious, or even shy, or nervous, or surprised, or a little bit afraid of someone you don't know yet or who looks different from you.

Hi, I'm Gus. This juggler's so cool!

If you do play with each other, you might find out that something he or she thinks is scary is something you think is scary. Or you might find out that something you think is silly is something he or she thinks is silly. And before you know it—you're talking, laughing, and having fun with each other.

You may notice that you and someone else have a different color or shade of skin or that something else about the two of you is the same or is different. You may even end up talking about what's different or the same.

But sometimes a person may say something not nice or mean about the color or shade of a person's skin, or the kind of hair or eyes a person has, or the way a person talks. Or about the clothes a person is wearing, or the people in a person's family, or how short or tall someone is, or the kind of food another person eats.

Everybody has feelings. That's one of the things that's the same for all of us.

We have happy feelings and sometimes we have sad or mad or bad feelings. Saying mean things to a person, calling someone a bad name, or laughing at or teasing that person can make that person feel very sad or even very mad.

A person who has been mean may feel very sad about what he or she has done. Saying "I'm sorry" can help the person he or she has been mean to feel better. It can also help the person who was being mean feel better. Treating people the way they want to be treated—and the way you want to be treated—can help everybody feel better.

Another thing that's the same about all of us is that everybody was a baby once. But even new babies are not always alike. Some are bigger. Some are smaller. Some have loud cries. And some have quiet cries.

Kids are not always alike. And grown-ups are not always alike. Some of us are quiet. Some of us are noisy. Some of us are shorter. Some of us are taller. Some of us like to eat pizza. Some of us like to eat rice and beans. Some of us like to have one friend. Some of us like to have lots of friends.

All of us—families and friends, girls and boys, men and women, babies, kids, and grown-ups—are alike and different in lots of ways. And everyone we know—even people we don't know and even people all around the world—are different and alike in lots of ways.

What's so wonderful is that all of us are more the same than we are different. What's so amazing is that no matter who you are, or how you look, or where you live—there is still only one of you!

Yes, Gus. I am ME. And you are YOU.

It's true, Nellie. You are YOU. And I am ME.

And that's WHO WE ARE!